PREPARING FOR

First Reconciliation

A GUIDE FOR FAMILIES

ELAINE MAHON

VERITAS

Published 2012 by Veritas Publications
7–8 Lower Abbey Street, Dublin 1, Ireland
publications@veritas.ie
www.veritas.ie

ISBN 978-1-84730-400-1

For my godsons, PJ, Joshua and Tom, in the hope that they will always trust in God's never-ending love.

Illustrations pages 7–10, 15 & 21 by Mary Cawley and Lir Mac Cárthaigh

The Story of the Prodigal Son is taken from *The Beginner's Bible: Timeless Bible Stories*, Candle Books, 2005

'When You Thought I Wasn't Looking' by Mary Rita Schilke Korzan is taken from *When You Thought I Wasn't Looking: A Book of Thanks for Mom* by Mary Rita Schilke Korzan, Andrews McMeel Publishing, 2004

10 9 8 7 6

A catalogue record for this book is available from the British Library.

Designed by Lir Mac Cárthaigh, Veritas
Printed in Ireland by Walsh Colour Print, Kerry

Veritas books are printed on paper made from the wood pulp of managed forests. For every tree felled, at least one tree is planted, thereby renewing natural resources.

1. I am Part of God's Family, and God Loves Me

Preparing for First Reconciliation is an important step on your child's journey of faith. This journey began on the day your child was baptised. Recall the promises you made on that day:

Parents, you have asked to have your child baptised. In doing so you are accepting the responsibility of training him/her in the practice of the faith. It will be your duty to bring him/her up to keep God's commandments as Christ taught us, by loving God and our neighbour. Do you clearly understand what you are undertaking?

Helping your child to prepare for the Sacrament of Reconciliation is perhaps an appropriate time for you to think again about their life of faith, and to look at how you are accepting the responsibilities that you took on during their Baptism. The following pages will help you to discuss your child's Baptism with them. You can also encourage your child to ask other family members and friends, including their godparents, about their Baptism. This will help your child to realise that they are part of both a loving, caring family and a wider community of faith.

A Prayer for Parents and Families

Loving God,
Thank you for the gift of _____ (your child's name).
As we remember the day we brought _____ to your church for Baptism, help us to fulfil our commitment to pass on the gift of faith to him/her.
May he/she grow in love for you and for others.
Amen.

When you were a baby, we made **lots of choices** for you:

Your name

What you wore

Where you lived

One of the choices that we made for you was that you would be **part of God's family**. We made this choice for you at your Baptism. Do you know …

Who was there on the day of your Baptism?

Who chose your name, or names, and why?

On that day, we also chose **godparents** to help you to get to know God as you grow up. Godparents are people who love you and care for you, and who want the best for you. Do you know …

Who are your godparents?

Why were they chosen as your godparents?

Do you have a photo of your Baptism? Stick it in this box.

When you were baptised, you became part of **God's family**. God has a very big family of millions and millions of people spread all over the world. We often talk about God being like the father or mother of this big family, and we are like his children – like brothers and sisters.

One of the first things that we learn about being part of this family is that **God loves us**. Since the very minute that you were born – and even before that – God has loved you. God loves everyone. Think of all the things that God has given to you:

Family to love and take care of you

Teachers to help you to learn

Friends to play with

God gave you all these things because God loves you and **God wants you to be happy**. God hopes that nothing will ever get between him and you.

PJ Prayer

Loving God,
Thank you for my parents and family,
who wanted me to be part of your Church.
Bless them and help them to keep teaching me about your love.
Keep us all safe through the night.
Amen.

2. The Parable of The Prodigal Son

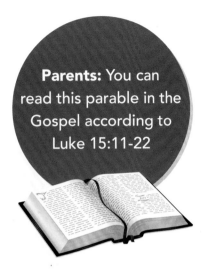

Parents: You can read this parable in the Gospel according to Luke 15:11-22

In everything he did and everything he said, Jesus tried to help people understand that our God is a God of love, compassion and forgiveness. Jesus demonstrated this by welcoming those who were outcast, by healing those who were sick, and by telling people parables like The Good Shepherd and The Prodigal Son.

In the pages that follow, help your child to read through the story of The Prodigal Son. Discuss it together and consider the following points:

- When the son realised that he did wrong, he wanted to go back to his father. This is the beginning of a conversion, or change of heart. At this point in the story, ask your child to think about times when they knew that they had done something wrong. Ask your child if it is easy to admit that they did something wrong. Share your own experiences.
- The father is overjoyed to see his son return. We see his happiness expressed in the robe, ring and banquet that he gives to his son. Talk to your child about a time when you were forgiven, and ask them to share their own experience of forgiveness.

A Prayer for Parents and Families

Loving God,
Thank you for your gifts of love and forgiveness.
Help us to demonstrate these gifts to our children,
so that they may be people of love, compassion and tolerance.
Amen.

Jesus told lots of stories. He told stories so that people would understand more about God and who God is. One of Jesus' most famous stories is about a father and his son. It is from the Gospel of Saint Luke.

The Prodigal Son

There was once a man who had two sons. He owned a big farm.

His youngest son did not want to work anymore. He wanted to travel and have fun. So he asked his father for his share of the family money.

The son got the money. He packed his things and left. He couldn't wait to see the world! His family was sad to see him go.

At first he had fun spending the money. He bought expensive clothes, and he ate fancy food.

But soon all the money was gone.

He had to go to work and he got a job with a pig farmer. He was so hungry that even the pigs' food looked good.

The son wanted to go back home. He said, 'I will tell my father I am sorry for what I have done. I do not deserve to be called his son. Maybe he will let me work for him.'

The father saw his son coming down the road. His eyes filled with tears as he ran to greet him.

The son said, 'Please forgive me, Dad.'

That night, they had a big party. The father said, 'My son was lost, but now he is found.'

Think about this story from **two different points of view**:

The Son

- How did he act at the start of the story?
- How did he feel when he realised that he had made a mistake?
- How did he feel when he saw his father coming towards him?

The Father

- How did he feel when the son said that he was leaving?
- Why did he give his son what he wanted? Why didn't he say no?
- How did the father feel when he saw his son coming home?

What words would you use to describe the father?

Who does the father remind you of?

When Jesus told this story, he was thinking about God. Jesus knew that God loves everyone, and that God wants everyone to be happy. He knew that God always forgives people when they realise that they need to say sorry for having done something wrong. **For Jesus, God is like the father in the story**.

Do you think God is like the father in the story?

PJ Prayer

Loving God,
Thank you for sending us your son, Jesus, to teach us about your love for us.
Help me to understand that you are like a caring mother or father, who always loves me.
Keep us all safe through the night.
Amen.

3. Turning Back to God

In the following pages we introduce children to the first step in the Sacrament of Reconciliation: Contrition. The first stage in any process of healing – be it religious or otherwise – is to recognise that there is something for which we are sorry. In preparation for the Sacrament of Reconciliation, we use an Examination of Conscience to help us to look at our lives and to identify those parts of it that are in need of healing.

In the beginning, you will need to take time to go through this exercise with your child, to help them to identify times when they didn't act as they should. As they grow older and more used to the celebration of the sacrament, they can do it by themselves. When reading the Examination of Conscience as your PJ Prayer this evening, your child may (or may not!) want to share some of their thoughts with you. If your child chooses to share aloud, listen attentively and affirm those times when they acted appropriately. Reassure them in their efforts to improve. You can finish with a hug and kiss, and perhaps just a comment, such as, 'I love you, and God loves you too.'

A Prayer for Parents and Families

Loving God,
Help our family to explore the difference between right and wrong with our children.
May they always feel that they can talk to us about the things for which they are sorry.
Give us the strength and courage to guide our children as they grow in relationship with you and with others.
Amen.

When the younger son in the story of the Prodigal Son knew that he had done something wrong, and when he was ready to say sorry, he turned around and started to make his way home.

Sometimes we say or do things that are wrong, or that hurt others. When we realise that we have done something wrong, and when we are ready to say that we are sorry, we also turn back to God. And just like the father in the story who was ready to welcome his son home, **God is always ready to welcome us back**.

Remember that no matter where you are, or what you are doing, you can talk to God. You don't even need to go to a church. **You can just close your eyes and talk to God** using your inside voice that no one else can hear. You can tell God about your day, or say 'Thank you' to God for something great that happened. You can ask God for help, or ask God to bless someone you know. You can also tell God if you are sorry for something that you did, or something that you didn't do.

There is, however, one very special way to say 'Sorry' to God, and that is by celebrating the **Sacrament of Reconciliation**. This year is an important year for you, because you will celebrate the Sacrament of Reconciliation for the very first time. You will be able to tell God that you are sorry for the times when you didn't live as Jesus asked us to, and God will help you to try harder next time. Close your eyes and listen carefully to these questions. Think about each one of them carefully.

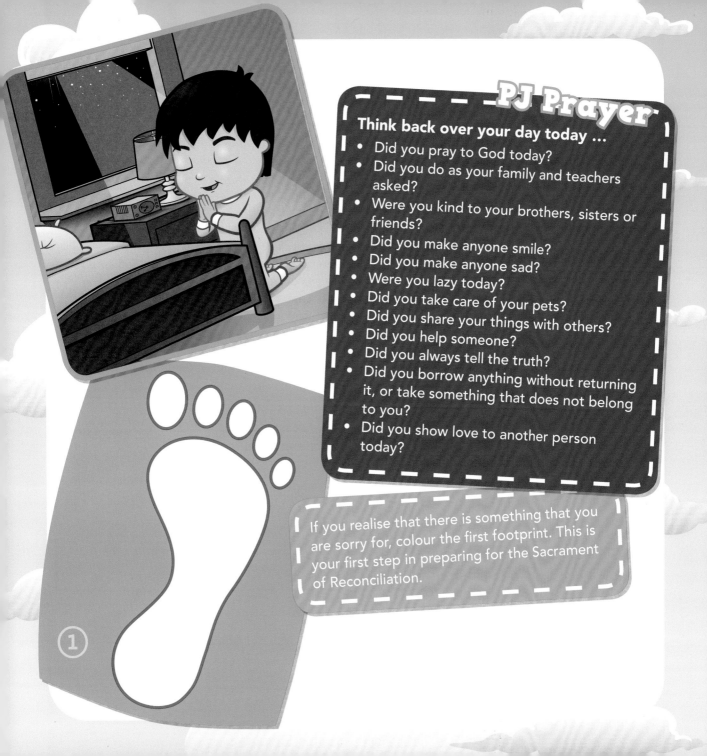

PJ Prayer

Think back over your day today ...

- Did you pray to God today?
- Did you do as your family and teachers asked?
- Were you kind to your brothers, sisters or friends?
- Did you make anyone smile?
- Did you make anyone sad?
- Were you lazy today?
- Did you take care of your pets?
- Did you share your things with others?
- Did you help someone?
- Did you always tell the truth?
- Did you borrow anything without returning it, or take something that does not belong to you?
- Did you show love to another person today?

If you realise that there is something that you are sorry for, colour the first footprint. This is your first step in preparing for the Sacrament of Reconciliation.

1

4. The Sacrament of Reconciliation

This section and the section that follows will help you to explain to your child what will happen when they celebrate the Sacrament of Reconciliation. Practices vary from parish to parish, so if you have any specific questions about what will happen on the day of your child's First Reconciliation, check with the priest or your child's teacher.

In celebrating the Sacrament of Reconciliation, our emphasis is always on the never-ending love and forgiveness of God, and so children need not be anxious or worried about celebrating the sacrament for the first time. However, if your child is particularly shy or nervous about talking to the priest, think about asking them to draw a picture showing a time when they didn't live as Jesus asks. They can bring this to the priest, and talk to him about it. All the time reassure your child of God's love – and indeed your love – for them.

A Prayer for Parents and Families

Loving God,
Help us to prepare our children for a sincere and honest confession.
May they never be afraid to admit when they have made a mistake, and to ask for forgiveness from you and from others.
Amen.

We have already seen how to get ready for the Sacrament of Reconciliation – by thinking about our lives and remembering those times when we didn't act the way God wants us to. Now it's time for the second step – telling the priest what we did that we want to say sorry for.

Colour the second footprint to show that you are ready for this next step.

②

How to celebrate the Sacrament of Reconciliation

① When you sit next to the priest, make the **Sign of the Cross** to show that you are there in God's name.

② Begin by telling the priest why you are there: **'Bless me, Father, for I have sinned.'** Then we tell the priest how long it has been since we last celebrated the Sacrament of Reconciliation. If it is your First Confession, you can tell him so.

What will you say to the priest on the day of your First Confession?

In the name of the _____ and of the _____ and of the _____ _____. Amen.

Bless me, Father _____ _____ _____ _____.

This is my _____ _____.

③ It's then time to tell the priest **what you are sorry for**. Remember that God loves you no matter what. You can be honest as you talk about what you have done wrong. God will always forgive you. You also don't need to worry that the priest will tell anyone. He will not. And he will never give out to you because you did something wrong. He just hears that you are sorry, and that you will try your very best in the future to live in the way that Jesus asks.

PJ Prayer

Confiteor

I confess to almighty God
and to you, my brothers and sisters,
that I have greatly sinned
in my thoughts and in my words,
in what I have done
and in what I have failed to do,
through my fault, through my fault,
through my most grievous fault;
therefore I ask blessed Mary ever-Virgin,
all the Angels and Saints,
and you, my brothers and sisters,
to pray for me to the Lord our God. Amen.

5. Penance

Penance can be defined as '... an act which shows that you feel sorry about something that you have done.' Children will be used to showing that they are sorry to siblings or friends after they have fallen out. As your child prepares for the Sacrament of Reconciliation, encourage them to continue to do little acts of penance. You can prompt them just by asking questions such as, 'What do you think you can do to make it up to your brother?' or 'How do you think you can show Nana that you are sorry?' That way, the penance they receive from the priest can be understood as another way for them to express sorrow.

A Prayer for Parents and Families

Loving God,
Guide us in helping our children to understand how they can make up for what they have done wrong through acts of penance and acts of kindness.
Help us to be role models for our children.
Amen.

After you have told the priest about the times when you did not live as Jesus asks, the priest might have a chat with you about some of the things that you said to him. Then **he will give you something to do to show that you are sorry** and that you want to make up for what you have done wrong. We call this a penance. Our penance might be to say a prayer, or to do something nice for someone that we have upset, or to go without something that we like.

We often try to 'make it up' to someone if we do something wrong. Think about it …

Imagine that you called your sister or brother a mean name when you were fighting. Later on, you were sorry for what you said. How might you make up for it?

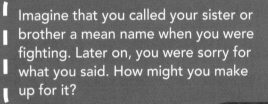

Imagine that you pushed your friend, who was annoying you, and his sweets fell on the ground. Later on, you felt bad about what you did. How might you make up for it?

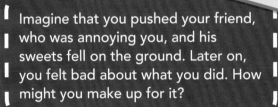

It is important that we say sorry to the people we have hurt. We can come up with our own ways to show others that we are sorry for hurting them.

If the priest asks us to say prayers for our penance, it is important that we **think really hard** as we say them. Think about what you did wrong as you say the words, and think about why you behaved in this way. If you hurt someone else, think about them as you say your prayer, and ask God to bless them.

Colour the third footprint if you are ready to do penance to show you are sorry for what you did wrong.

③

PJ Prayer

Loving God,
I know that when I do something wrong,
I am not the person that you want me to be.
Help me to show you that I am sorry.
Help me to show others that I am sorry too.
Help me not to sin again.
Keep us all safe through the night.
Amen.

6. I say I am Sorry and I am Forgiven

The Act of Sorrow that your child is learning may be a different version to the version that you learned when you were preparing for your First Reconciliation, or indeed to the one you say today. It is a beautiful prayer. Spend some time looking though it line by line with your child, helping them to understand the meaning of the words.

As you move on to discuss Absolution and forgiveness with your child, recall how healing and Reconciliation were such an important part of the life of Jesus. He, as the Son of God, forgave sins. We believe that the same forgiveness is today available to us through the Sacrament of Reconciliation.

The Sacrament of Reconciliation is a mystery, and so neither adults nor children will ever be able to fully understand it. Our role as parents/guardians and family members is not to explain the Sacrament of Reconciliation so perfectly that our children no longer have any questions! Rather, our duty is to help children to understand as best they can, to ask questions, and to continue to grow in friendship with Jesus.

A Prayer for Parents and Families

Loving God,
Thank you for the gift of this sacrament.
Help us to see it as an opportunity to be reconciled with you and with others. Help us to teach this to our children.
Amen.

When you have finished talking with the priest, and after he has spoken to you about penance, he will ask you to say a prayer called the **Act of Sorrow**. This shows that you are truly sorry, and that you want to try harder. Look at each line of the prayer and think about what it means.

> O my God,
> I thank you for loving me.

We begin the prayer by **thanking God** for loving us. God will always love you. Nothing you ever do will make God stop loving you. He loves you like a mother or father.

> I am sorry for all my sins,

Next, **we tell God that we are sorry** for the things that we have done wrong. God will always forgive us.

> for not loving others and not loving you.

These are two things that Jesus asked us to do – **to love God and to love other people**. We are sorry for the times when we didn't do these two things.

> Help me to live like Jesus and not sin again. Amen.

We should never give up trying **to live in the way that Jesus wants**. We need God's help to do this.

After you have said the Act of Sorrow, the priest will say **a special blessing called an Absolution** over you. He may put his hand over your head or raise his arm as he is saying the Absolution.

This blessing shows us that **God has welcomed us back**, just like the father in the story of The Prodigal Son. Like the younger son, we have said that we made mistakes, that we are sorry, and that we will try not to make the same mistake again. God wants us to be happy, and to make others happy. That is why God wants us to try our best to live like Jesus.

Colour the fourth footprint if you would like to receive Absolution from the priest.

④

PJ Prayer

Act of Sorrow

O my God,
I thank you for loving me,
I am sorry for all my sins,
for not loving others and not loving you.
Help me to live like Jesus and not sin again.
Amen.

7. I Try Again

The Sacrament of Reconciliation always ends with our promise to live a better life. Obviously, this is no easy task! As parents/guardians and family members, we know that children learn by example. They learn how to show love when they witness your acts of kindness for your family. They learn about Reconciliation when they watch you forgive. They learn about hope when they see that you don't give up easily. Think about the following poem:

When you thought I wasn't looking,
You hung my first painting on the refrigerator
And I wanted to paint another one.

When you thought I wasn't looking,
You fed a stray cat,
And I thought it was good to be kind to animals.

When you thought I wasn't looking,
You baked a birthday cake just for me,
And I knew that little things were special things.

When you thought I wasn't looking,
You said a prayer,
And I believed there is a God I could always talk to.

When you thought I wasn't looking,
You kissed me good-night,
And I felt loved.

When you thought I wasn't looking,
I saw tears come from your eyes,
And I learned that sometimes things hurt –
But it's all right to cry.

When you thought I wasn't looking,
You smiled,
And it made me want to look that pretty too.

When you thought I wasn't looking,
You cared,
And I wanted to be everything I could be.

When you thought I wasn't looking,
I looked ...
And I wanted to say 'thanks'
For all those things you did
When you thought I wasn't looking.

Mary Rita Schilke Korzan

In the following pages we ask children to think about things that they can do to live as a friend of Jesus. You can also add your own ideas. Over the coming days and weeks, notice when your child does some of these things, and remind them that they are living the way Jesus asked.

A Prayer for Parents and Families

Loving God,
Help us to recommit ourselves to doing your will, especially after the celebration of the Sacrament of Reconciliation.
Give us the strength to be positive role models for our children and for each other.
Amen.

After we celebrate the Sacrament of Reconciliation, **our sins are forgiven**. Our job may not be finished, though. There may be people that we still need to say sorry to.

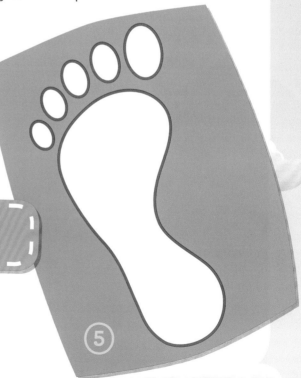

If we have hurt or upset anyone, or if there is someone we are fighting with, **we need to make sure that we say sorry**, and that we try to make up with them.

The last line of the Act of Sorrow is, 'Help me to live like Jesus and not sin again'. So every time we celebrate the Sacrament of Reconciliation, we try our best once again **to act as friends of Jesus**, by loving God and loving other people.

Colour the final footprint if you are ready to try again.

⑤

In the circles below, you can read some ideas for ways in which **you can live like a friend of Jesus**. Try your best to do these things at all times, but especially after you have celebrated the Sacrament of Reconciliation. Each time you do one of these nice things, colour in the circle. See if you can colour them all!

Be patient at times when you have to wait

Give something to charity

Say Grace Before Meals

Say you are sorry when you do something wrong

Share what you have with others

Play with someone who has been left out

Pay attention at Mass

PJ Prayer

Loving God,
Help me to try my best at all times to live like
  your son, Jesus.
Help me to decide on the right thing to do
  when I have a choice to make.
Bless my teachers, priests, parents and family,
  and all who help me to be the best person
  I can be.
Keep us all safe through the night.
Amen.

8. How I Reconcile With God and With Others

We hope that you have enjoyed reading this book with your child, and that you have learned something about the Sacrament of Reconciliation yourself. Preparing for the sacraments is a special and important time for parents and families, and one to be treasured. It is important to remember, however, that Reconciliation is a life-long process, and that the Sacrament of Reconciliation is one that we are encouraged to engage in throughout our lives. It is a sad reality that many people experience this sacrament just a couple of times as children and then never again. It is important that families build a regular Reconciliation routine into their prayer life, so that children know that it is something to be valued. Many families choose to participate in parish Reconciliation services, which often happen during Advent and again during Lent. This is a pattern that children can continue into their teenage years and into adulthood.

It is also important that adults can be role models for children when it comes to the Sacrament of Reconciliation. If, by reading this book, you think that the Sacrament of Reconciliation is something that you want for your child, ask yourself if it is something that you want for yourself. If you haven't celebrated the Sacrament of Reconciliation for many years, you may have some understandable concerns or nervousness about it. Consider talking to your priest about this before you present yourself for the sacrament. Address your unease, and remember what you have told your child and what we have said in this book: God is Love.

… while he was still far off, his father saw him and was filled with compassion; he ran and put his arms around him and kissed him. (Luke 15:20)

A Prayer for Parents and Families

Loving God,
Help us to trust in your forgiveness.
May our children always know and believe in your loving presence in their lives.
Keep them safe, healthy and happy.
Amen.

You have come to the end of the journey in preparing for the Sacrament of Reconciliation.

Remember the five footsteps that you coloured:

1. I realise I am _____.
2. I tell the _____ about what I did wrong.
3. I do my _____.
4. God _____ me.
5. I _____ again.

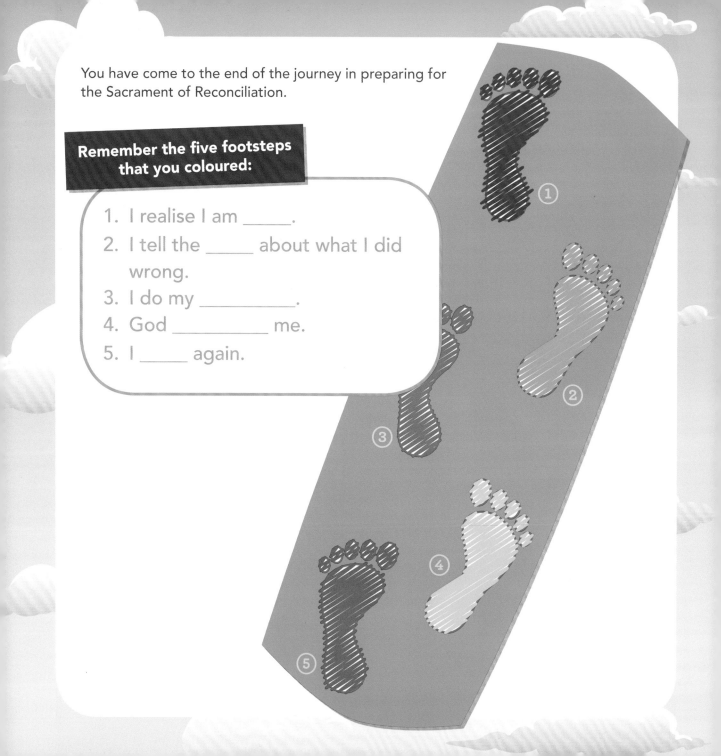

Fill in the certificate at the end of this book to help you remember the first time you celebrated the Sacrament of Reconciliation. Try your best to **celebrate this sacrament as often as you can**, and especially when you are getting ready to celebrate Jesus' birthday at Christmastime and his Resurrection at Eastertime. Remember that God is always there for you. God will always forgive you. God always loves you.

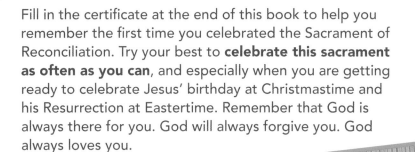

PJ Prayer

Loving God,
Thank you for my parents and family, for my teachers and priests, and for all who teach me about you.
Help me to live as your friend.
Help me to be sorry for those times when I do not live as I should.
I know I can always turn back to you.
Help me to do that.
Keep me safe through the night. Amen.

For you to cut out and keep

Certificate of First Reconciliation

Awarded to

....
Write your name here

I celebrated my First Reconciliation on

....
Write the date

Stick a photo of yourself in this box.

These people helped me to prepare:

....
My Family

....
My Teacher

....
My Priest